VIRU'S PMP TWEETS

VIRU'S PMP TWEETS

Virupakshan Krishnamoorthi

PARTRIDGE

To order additional copies of this book, contact
Partridge India
000 800 10062 62
orders.india@partridgepublishing.com

www.partridgepublishing.com/india

TOPICS COVERED

A. Organization 1

B. Employee 3

C. Customer 5

D. Project 7

E. Project Management 9

F. Project Scope 11

G. Project Estimation 13

H. Project Schedule 15

I. Project Planning 17

J. Project Team 19

K. Project Execution 21

L. Risk Management 23

M. Process 25

N. Tools 27

O. Training 29

P. Leadership 31

Q. Quality 33

R. Communication 35

S. Business Enabler 37

T. Motivation 39

U. Policies 41

V. Managing Change 43

W. Innovation 45

X. Knowledge Management 47

Y. Appraisal 49

Z. Work Life Balance 51

DEDICATED TO

MY THREE ROLE MODELS

Prof. Sp. Veerapandian   **Prof. R. Ananthan**   **Mr. B. Narayan**

Great Humanitarian   Great Educationist   Great Professional

PREFACE

If you wish to get some quick idea about "Project Management Principles", then read this book.

If you are looking for complete knowledge about Project Management, then http://www.pmi.org/ is the place – as far as I know.

You can connect with me here:

TWITTER	FACEBOOK	EMAIL
@virupa	fb.com/virupa	virupa@Kart.La

A

ORGANIZATION

1. An organization involved in supply of goods and/or services to consumers is an important organ in the economic system.

2. The organization that creates value for customers, employees, investors and all stakeholders will be respected.

3. An organization that is honest, legal and ethical alone can grow with respect in the long run.

4. An organization that uses technology, is innovative & manages change alone can sustain and grow.

B

EMPLOYEE

1. Employees are the real assets of an organization and not any other material resources.

2. Good employees grow the organization while not-so-good employees bring it down.

3. An organization can achieve its mission and vision only when it's employees buy-in to those mission & vision.

4. Organizations that keep their employees motivated & satisfied can easily satisfy their customers and stakeholders.

C

CUSTOMER

1. An organization exists only because their customers exist and this must be remembered all the time.

2. Most customers want their problem solved through high quality, long lasting and economical solution.

3. An organization can succeed only when it understands customer problems and provides the apt solution.

4. Why some employees, who are customers to other organizations, don't try to understand their own customers?

D

PROJECT

1. Organizations perform work through either operations or projects that are both planned, executed and controlled using limited resources.

2. Operations are ongoing & repetitive while projects are unique with definite start & end dates.

3. A project is a temporary endeavor undertaken to create a unique product or service or a desired result.

4. A project may involve one or more persons, units and partnering with other organizations.

E

PROJECT MANAGEMENT

1. Project Management is the application of knowledge, skills, tools & techniques to project activities to achieve project goals.

2. Managing scope, time, cost, quality, resources, risk, change, communication and procurement are important in Project Management.

3. Changing scope, availability of resources on time, communication problems and people challenges are critical issues faced by many project managers.

4. Why does senior management in some organizations review and guide a project only after customer escalation?

F

PROJECT SCOPE

1. Project Scope refers to the work that must be done to deliver a product or service with specific features and functions.

2. Before starting a project, the requestor/customer and project team should agree to all terms defined in a Scope Statement.

3. Scope Statement includes features & functions, acceptance criteria, deliverables, exclusions and assumptions.

4. Improper scope management may lead to scope creep; effort, cost & schedule overruns and strained relationships.

G

PROJECT ESTIMATION

1. Estimating effort & cost for a project is extremely critical and hence must use the right methods, tools & people to do it.

2. Unclear scope may drastically affect the estimation, irrespective of the methods, tools and techniques used.

3. Estimating just to win a contract may harm both the organization and the customer.

4. Why some people who estimate for a project never get involved once the project starts?

H

PROJECT SCHEDULE

1. Schedule mainly depends on scope, resources availability, team experience, task dependencies, project complexity, cultural and physical environment.

2. A realistic schedule considers not only declared holidays, but also team member's leaves, non-project activities and unexpected/unplanned events.

3. Unrealistic schedule may do more harm than unrealistic estimate for both the organization and the customer.

4. Proper inputs, tools, techniques and reviews help in preparing a realistic project schedule.

I

PROJECT PLANNING

1. Project planning is to document scope, estimate work, create schedule, document risk management, define quality standards and do staffing plan.

2. Project plan is used to guide project execution, document assumptions, milestones & decisions made and facilitate communication among all.

3. Project plan should be expected to change over time as more information becomes available about the project.

4. It is difficult to execute and control a project without reviewing and updating the project plan on a regular basis.

J
PROJECT TEAM

1. Project team must be formed with right set of people in different roles, in the right ratio.

2. Project team formation must be done considering the skill requirement and also the project's profit margin.

3. Selecting too many experienced or inexperienced members for a project may have its own adverse effects.

4. A good project team is one in which hierarchy is followed but not felt.

K

PROJECT EXECUTION

1. For project execution to be successful, a project leader should assign people with the right skills and passion for different types of tasks.

2. Understanding the entire scope and contributing their part with high quality is the responsibility of a good team member.

3. Managing & developing team, performing tasks & reviews, increasing performance & quality and communicating with all stake holders are project leader's responsibility.

4. What can go wrong in a project if there is a perfect plan, good team, necessary resources, good leaders & understanding customer?

L

RISK MANAGEMENT

1. Risk Identification, Qualitative & Quantitative Analysis, Response Planning, Monitoring and Controlling are important in Risk Management.

2. Historic inputs, tacit knowledge and group reviews help in good Risk Management.

3. Avoidance, transference, mitigation and acceptance are the response plans for Project Risk Management.

4. Failure to monitor and control risks during a project may lead to effort, schedule and cost overruns.

M

PROCESS

1. A project without a process is like a language without a grammar.

2. Initiating, Planning, Executing, Controlling and Closing Processes have to be followed in each project.

3. It may be difficult to learn a process initially, but once learnt, it would be more difficult to unlearn.

4. Why do some projects follow a particular process methodology which does not benefit either the customer or the project team?

N

TOOLS

1. A project needs the right tools to manage, execute, communicate and collaborate.

2. A project without any tool is like a painter without a brush.

3. Investing time and money in buying or building a tool for a project must be done based on Return On Investment.

4. Why do some projects stick to old tools when new tools that are more efficient and easy to use are available?

O

TRAINING

1. Training an employee on a regular basis in various fields like technology, domain and behavior is important for the employee and the organization.

2. An apt methodology, a good trainer and proper training materials are extremely important for effective training.

3. Training must be in such a way that the trainee must say 'I want to learn' rather than 'I have to learn'.

4. A plant grows by itself - the gardener only creates an atmosphere for it to grow. Similarly, a trainer should only create an atmosphere for learning – the trainee will learn on his own.

P

LEADERSHIP

1. Honesty, Knowledge, Communication, Attitude, Ability to delegate & inspire, Sense of humor, Creativity and Commitment are important qualities of a good leader.

2. A good leader is neither aggressive nor submissive, but assertive with everyone most of the time.

3. Mostly employees don't leave their organization or department or team, but their managers who call themselves as leaders.

4. A great leader is identified not just by their number of followers but also by the number of leaders he/she created.

Q
QUALITY

1. Identifying relevant quality standards, regularly evaluating performance and monitoring & controlling project results for quality standards compliance are important.

2. Quality standards, checklists, apt tools, good plan and regular audits are useful only if the work results are proper.

3. Following process for achieving quality may irritate some but not following will frustrate both the team and the customer.

4. Is it better to conduct more audits for better adherence as some projects align to quality standards during audits?

R

COMMUNICATION

1. Successful people and organizations know "what, when, who and how" to communicate.

2. It is not "what you communicate" but "how you communicate it" is more important.

3. Like how Valluvar said, great people tell only what will be useful and don't tell anything that is useless.

4. Tools should make communication more effective and efficient. Unfortunately, some are used to flood redundant and useless information.

S

BUSINESS ENABLER

1. Members from other departments who directly or indirectly contribute to the success of a project are business enablers.

2. To understand the importance of business enablers in a project, just ask the facilities team not to work for a day.

3. For project team, customers are external to the organization and for business enablers, project team is their customer.

4. Personal rapport with business enablers work well if the firm is small but process with SLAs work even when it grows big.

T

MOTIVATION

1. A person who understands 'what motivates others' and takes action accordingly will be extremely successful.

2. Extrinsic motivation like money, status, etc. may be helpful for short term gains but intrinsic motivation is helpful for long term gains.

3. A highly motivated team with lesser skills is much better than a highly skilled team with lesser motivation.

4. Why many people like extrinsic motivation which gives both pain and joy instead of intrinsic motivation which gives only joy?

U

POLICIES

1. Good policies govern & help an organization to grow and not-so-good policies spoil its growth & most importantly reputation.

2. Good policy makers, before defining a policy, spend enough time to understand all consequences.

3. Removing outdated policies, modifying some old policies and adding new policies on a regular basis helps an organization to grow.

4. Can exceptions to policies handle those employees who mostly use policies to avoid doing a good work?

V

MANAGING CHANGE

1. Those who understand "Why, What & How to change" & strategize can grow faster and others may not grow or become obsolete.

2. It is human nature to resist change and hence managing change in an organization must be well planned & executed.

3. Open & honest communication, getting a buy-in from employees and allowing enough time for people to adapt are important in managing change.

4. Why some organizations treat change/transformation as an event rather than a mental, physical and emotional process?

W

INNOVATION

1. Innovation is doing something different rather than doing the same thing better - so that it breaks in to a market or society.

2. Innovation is the only differentiator for long-term growth and success of an organization.

3. Some organizations, which doesn't realize that almost every human is innovative, search for innovators outside instead of creating an ecosystem for their employees inside.

4. Isn't is surprising to see some organizations, which asks their employees to innovate 'at gun point', succeed?

X

KNOWLEDGE MANAGEMENT

1. Knowledge Management comprises a range of strategies & practices used in an organization to identify, create, represent, distribute and enable adoption of insights & experiences.

2. A good Knowledge Management system has good tools, processes and employee engagement mechanism.

3. Knowledge Management will be effective only if rewards for sharing, reviewing and consuming such shared knowledge are good.

4. What is the purpose in spending time & money for Knowledge Management if most employees seek outside knowledge instead of inside knowledge?

Y

APPRAISAL

1. A good appraisal system is simple, objective, motivating and provides constructive feedback to all members.

2. Proper & practical goal setting and regular recording of feedbacks & evaluations achieve a highly objective appraisal.

3. As we are all humans, how much ever objectivity dominates, at least a little subjectivity may decide the appraisal outcome.

4. How does an appraisal system handle the fact that people are not afraid of failures but insults arising out of such failures?

Z

WORK LIFE BALANCE

1. Setting proper expectations in both personal & official life and acting accordingly helps in achieving work-life balance.

2. Clear objective, Planning, Prioritizing, Managing time and Interpersonal skills are important to achieve work-life balance.

3. Like how a project may need your dedicated focus for some time when others can't help in a particular situation, your family may also need your focus.

4. Is it possible to achieve a good work-life balance without any sort of compromise?

About the Author

1. Virupakshan or Virupa or Viru – holds B.Sc.(Physics), B.Tech. (Automobile Engineering) and M.B.A. (Project Management) degrees.

2. He got 12+ years of experience in Infosys, had short stints in Cognizant & MindTree, learned many lessons in his first entrepreneurial attempt and learning many more in his second entrepreneurial attempt through www. Kart.La platform.

3. He is passionate about bringing equality among humans (influence of Prof. Sp. Veerapandian – a great Humanitarian), changing the education system in such a way that people would say "I want to learn" instead of "I have to learn" (influence of Prof. R. Ananthan - a great Educationist) and helping customers & business owners by leveraging science & technology (influence of Mr. B. Narayan – a great Professional)

4. He is looking for honest, mature and wise people to invest in his start-up company "KARTLA SOLUTIONS PRIVATE LIMITED" which is developing a platform www.Kart.La to bring all Local Area shops online.

www.ingramcontent.com/pod-product-compliance
Lightning Source LLC
Chambersburg PA
CBHW021917170526
45157CB00005B/2091